Portland Community College Libraries

WITHDRAWN

16

THE OPEN MEDIA PAMPHLET SERIES

D0190709

Portland Community College Library

THE OPEN MEDIA PAMPHLET SERIES

The Last Energy War

The Battle Over Utility Deregulation

HARVEY WASSERMAN

SEVEN STORIES PRESS / New York

Copyright © 1999 by Harvey Wasserman

A Seven Stories Press First Edition,
published in association with Open Media.

Open Media Pamphlet Series editors,
Greg Ruggiero and Stuart Sahulka.

All rights reserved. No part of this book may
be reproduced, stored in a retrieval system, or transmitted in any form,
by any means, including mechanical, electric, photocopying, recording
or otherwise, without the prior written permission of the publisher.

Library of Congress Cataloging-in-Publication Data

Wasserman, Harvey.
    The last energy war: the battle of utility deregulation / Harvey
Wasserman.
    p.   cm. — (Open media pamphlet series: v. 16)
ISBN: 1-58322-017-8 (pbk.)
    1. Electric utilities—Deregulation—United States. I. Title. II. Series.
HD9685.U5W38 1999
333.793'2'0973—dc21   99-39622
                                                       CIP

Book design by Cindy LaBreacht
9 8 7 6 5 4 3 2 1
Printed in the U.S.A.

THIS IS DEDICATED TO THE WIND I LOVE.

CONTENTS

Acknowledgments

The fight for ecological survival, green energy and public power is a collaborative effort, as is this book. Special thanks to Anna Aurelio, Jaron Bourke, Jon Broder, Eugene Coyle, Scott Denman, Mark Dowie, Paul Fenn, Paul Gunter, Herb and Elizabeth Gunther, Wenonah Hauter, Mark Hertsgaard, Charlie Higley, Charles Komanoff, Paul Rogat Loeb, Mark Loy, Michael Mariotte, Dick Munson, Ralph Nader, Christine Patronic-Holder, Bonnie Raitt, Jim Riccio, John Richards, Harvey Rosenfield, Jason Salzman, Norman Solomon, John Tirman, and so many more who read the manuscript in its various forms and provided key help by word and deed, but are in no way responsible for its shortcomings. Dan Berman, as always, went above and beyond the call of duty. Susan, Rachel, Annie, Abbie, Julie and Shoshanna, Joiwind and Amit, Journey and Sarah, give it all meaning.

Prologue: Showdown at Diablo

On a brilliant sun-drenched afternoon in the mid 1980s, more than a decade of grassroots organizing against the Diablo Canyon nuclear plant drew to a climax. Scores of protesters were dragged off the road leading up to the huge twin reactor domes that dominate the dramatic seascape north of Avila Beach, halfway between San Francisco and Los Angeles.

Those domes help form the explosive nucleus of electric power deregulation, the biggest corporate scam in the history of the United States. With the trillion-dollar failure of atomic energy at center stage, the restructuring of the U.S. utility industry represents the climax of more than a century of bitter struggle over control of the nation's source of electricity. The conflict now generated will help define a new millennium in economic and ecological survival.

Diablo's aptly named double reactors went critical not long after the last of more than 10,000 of us were arrested. We were outraged that Diablo had been built with mammoth cost overruns less than four miles from the Hosgri earthquake fault, known to be one of California's strongest and most active. A seismic crack could release enough radiation to forever destroy the fertile plains of central California. It could cost untold billions in property damage. By the government's own studies (done long before Chernobyl) it could contaminate and kill tens of thousands of downwind Americans.

Instead, we wanted an electric supply based on efficiency and renewables, especially solar power and wind energy, which were already making deep inroads in the California landscape. For two decades, we'd also argued that atomic energy was an economic mess, a conclusion now every bit as mainstream as the idea that the Vietnam war was a mistake. Comparing its costs to the space program and Vietnam combined, *Forbes Magazine* in 1985 termed nuclear power "the largest managerial disaster in business history...a defeat for the U.S. consumer and for the competitiveness of U.S. industry, for the utilities that undertook the program and for the private enterprise system that made it possible."

State police allowed us part way onto the site to avoid injuries along the busy intersecting coastal road. Then, one-by-one they jujitsued us out of our chanting circles. School buses took us to the San Luis Obispo County Jail, where we spent three nights in orange polyester. Then we spoke to an emotional public hearing in front of the district's Democratic Congressman Leon Panetta (later Bill Clinton's White House Chief of Staff).

But PG&E soon forced Diablo on line. America's biggest private utility had lavished more than $5 billion in the project. It had never been put to a public vote. It had survived Three Mile Island. It weathered global embarrassment when a last-minute review (prompted by the protests) showed that critical blueprints had been misread.

For PG&E dominated California politics. Its tentacles reached deep into the state's highest financial and legislative circles. What PG&E wanted, it got.

And it wanted Diablo Canyon on line.

A decade later, PG&E and its sibling utilities, in the name of "competition," wanted to stick the public with their failed nuclear experiment. They were besieged by plunging gas prices, and by rapid advances in solar and wind power. They saw a way to unload their bad reactor investments on the rate-paying public while grabbing gargantuan sums of cash. Led by a former environmentalist turned pro-nuclear utility baron, California's utilities blasted through a hundred years of regulatory history. They would cripple public oversight and public power. They would de-unionize their industry. They would transform themselves from public service providers to cash-rich buccaneers cruising global money markets, accountable to no one.

Above all, they would turn the trillion-dollar mistake of atomic energy into a gigantic money laundering machine that would also cripple the solar technologies poised to deliver safe, cheap, democratically controlled power to the American public.

The scheme to do all that is called "electric utility deregulation."

This is its story, from the beginning.

PART ONE: EARLY ELECTRONS

Chapter One:
Alternating Edison

Electricity was known to the ancient Greeks (as was the use of solar energy to heat houses). Some 600 years before Christ, a philosopher-mathematician named Thales rubbed a piece of amber with fur and produced a primitive version of alternating current—attracting and then repelling small objects.

Twenty-four centuries of experimentation later, Humphrey Davy turned that magic into an electric lamp. In the early 1800s the British scientist jumped a brilliant current between two carbon rods. By 1844 such lamps lit up the Paris Opera. Soon Michael Faraday, Davy's assistant, built a reliable generator, and documented many of the basic laws that define electricity.

In 1878, an Ohio inventor named Charles Brush, already renown for his work in telegraphy, perfected an arc lamp, and used it to light his Cleveland offices. Then at 8:05PM, April 29, 1879, Brush bathed the heart of Cleveland in blinding light from a dozen arc lamps perched on fifteen-foot poles. A huge crowd cheered in amazement. The Cleveland Grays band burst into song. Artillery boomed across the lakefront. A revolutionary new technology had been born, and with it a century of political struggle that still burns uniquely hot in Cleveland.

Brush quickly began charging the city a dollar an hour to light Cleveland. But in New York, Thomas Edison had his sights on bigger bucks.

Edison was the grandson of a wealthy Tory who fought against George Washington, then fled to Canada. Edison's father then tangled with the Canadian government, and eventually returned to the U.S.. Along his way to fame and fortune, young Tom blew up laboratories, bankrupted backers, and often took undue credit—and royalties—for lucrative advances associated with his name.

As inventor/entrepreneurs like Brush and Edison spread their lighting systems to city after city, they dragged banks, franchising operations and armies of lawyers and hack politicians in their wake. By the late 1880s, "nearly every city in the country had granted several general electric light franchises to competing electric companies," write Richard Rudolph and Scott Ridley in *Power Struggle*. "Out of a belief that maximum competition between the companies would keep charges low, some city governments granted franchises to all companies desiring to supply electric service."

This single decade of frontier-style chaos was the only time in U.S. history the electricity market could be termed "free."

Future advocates of deregulation would mythologize such competition.

But in practice, it was an unmitigated disaster: a short-term free-for-all, followed by an avalanche of corporate consolidation. In city after city, throughout the 1880s, poles and wires proliferated like weeds. Hundreds of small, underfunded entrepreneurs pasted together financing for generators, wires and lights, only to fall prey to lethal shortages of capital, expertise and integrity.

Then came the sharks. In Chicago, in 1887, the Gas Trust Company snapped up all the little fish. Its Arc Light and Power Company established "a monopoly of all the light with which Chicago is to be blessed." Everywhere, the story was much the same—except in New York, where the scale was bigger and the names better known. Buying into the area around Wall Street, Edison hooked up with J. Pierpont Morgan, the nation's premier banker, and began building the biggest of the electric empires.

Morgan avoided the frequent breakdowns of Edison's Pearl Street Station by installing a generator in his Fifth Avenue mansion. He also aimed to avoid the inconveniences of competition, which he considered barbaric, an unconscionable waste of resources. With his fellow Robber Barons—Cleveland's John D. Rockefeller in oil, James J. Hill in railroads, the Armours and Swifts in meat—Morgan turned the 1880s and 1890s from an era of frontier competition into one of consolidation and corporate control.

Morgan's vision of the electric power business was clear and simple: there would be one utility, owned by him. So Morgan built on Edison's patents, promoting Edison's name as the nascent telecommunications industry used the name of Alexander Graham Bell.

To neuter public opposition, Morgan bought off whole state legislatures. He penetrated deep into the most corrupt Congresses in U.S. history, run by what Mark Twain called America's only native "criminal class."

Edison was no financial genius, and Morgan soon took his tangible assets.

Edison also promoted direct (DC) current rather than

alternating (AC) current for moving mass quantities of electricity. But his former lab assistant, Nicola Tesla, persisted (correctly) in pushing AC, with backing from another early Robber Baron, George Westinghouse. Edison made a show of AC's dangers by using it to electrocute some 50 dogs and cats, which inspired the state of New York to install an AC electric chair. In August, 1890, William Kemmler died in it. Once a foe of the death penalty, Edison said the horribly maimed prisoner had been "Westinghoused."

Soon Edison diverted his inventive genius into telegraphy, the phonograph and motion picture technology. But the business of electric power exploded—along with the political warfare to control it. Sticking the Edison name on new utility systems sprouting throughout the U.S., Morgan sent General Electric on the road to becoming the world's largest corporation. Morgan, Westinghouse, the rising young Samuel Insull monopolized urban lighting, power and trolley systems. Their empires were integrated into the gigantic monopolies rising around the railroad, telecommunications, oil, shipping, food and other key businesses—all the choke points of an American industrial machine transforming into the world's largest. Soon they dwarfed the state and federal governments they thoroughly controlled.

But they were not without opposition.

Chapter Two:
Adding Injury to Insull

As Morgan and Westinghouse built their gargantuan fortunes, angry grassroots Americans demanded ownership of their own power supply. Starting with a Brush generator in Fairfield, Iowa, some 53 cities and towns established their own municipal systems by 1888. Over the next hundred years, such public systems—virtually without exception—would consistently deliver power more cheaply and reliably than those in baronial hands.

In 1893 the U.S. plunged into an economic disaster known until the 1930s as "the Great Depression." That spring, 15,282 Detroiters voted to establish a municipal generator to produce power under public control, exclusive of the private monopolies. Despite a massive campaign by Morgan's Detroit Electric Light and Power (whose chief engineer was Henry Ford), only 1,745 voted no. By 1895 the city had a "muni"—a municipally-owned utility. Populist Mayor Hazen Pingree said such public power put electricity "within reach of the humblest of citizens."

On one idea, public power advocates like Pingree actually agreed with Morgan—the utility business was a "natural monopoly." But Pingree thought it should be the property of the people. And wherever the people were in control, rates usually went down. The price of running a street lamp in Pingree's Detroit dropped from $132 per year in 1894 under private control to $63 per year in 1902 under municipal control. Ferocious battles for such benefits erupted in San Francisco, Toledo, Chicago, Cleveland and elsewhere. Munis everywhere offered cheaper rates and a political freedom unknown where private barons owned both the utility and the government.

Amidst the 1893-7 depression, powerful farm-labor movements amplified the demand for community control, not only of electric utilities, but of the banking, transportation, telecommunications and a wide range of affiliated industries. The Populist Party united black and white farmers of the south and west in a grassroots coalition that stood on the brink of national power, particularly after a strong showing in the presidential campaign of 1892. In 1894, the party surged ahead in state and local elections. Meanwhile a booming labor movement flirted with democratic socialism, particularly under the leadership of Eugene V. Debs, the Indiana unionist who sought to organize all working people. United, the Populist and Debsian movements might have reshaped 20th century social democracy. But in 1896, the Populists shattered amidst the confused and corrupted election of the baronial Republican William McKinley of Ohio. With the divisive defeat of William Jennings Bryan of Nebraska, the Populists fell into disarray.

But the demand for popular control of industrial empires like the electric utilities continued to surge forward. Throughout the 1890s and into the new century the rise of municipal electric systems challenged the ruling elite, especially in Cleveland.

"I believe in municipal ownership of these monopolies, because if you do not own them, they will in time own you," said populist Tom Johnson. "They will destroy your politics, corrupt your institutions, and, finally, destroy your liberties." Johnson was mayor from 1901-9. His sentiments defined Cleveland's electric politics all the way to "boy mayor" Dennis Kucinich in the 1970s and Michael White in the 1990s. (In 1998, as a U.S. Congressman, Kucinich presented the nation's most coherent blueprint for restructuring the electric utility industry along democratic lines).

In 1905 Johnson began an end run around the GE subsidiary that Morgan used to swallow up Charles Brush's pioneer street lights. Johnson tried to take over Cleveland Electric Light, but was blocked by a corrupt city council. So he won a referendum annexing the suburb of South Brooklyn, which had its own municipal plant. In 1911 the city voted for a $2 million bond issue to build a 24-megawatt, four-turbine public plant on the Lake Erie shore. Cleveland's Muni began selling juice in 1914. For nearly nine decades since, Cleveland Electric and its successors have tried to destroy it. But mayors like Kucinich and White have helped stop them.

Nationwide, between sixty and 120 new munis were formed every year from 1897 through 1907. By 1912 there were 3,659 private utilities, and 1,737 public ones. War raged between them. A community would propose a public utility to cut prices and restore democracy. Then the privates sent in an army of lawyers, politicians and public relations flaks. Years—sometimes decades—of bitter struggle followed.

But where munis flourished, rates dropped and service improved. In the wake of the Populist upheaval, and with the continuing rise of Debs and the labor and socialist movements, the race between public and private power remained very much up in the air.

Until Samuel Insull perfected a "third way." Insull's "progressive" brainchild was a private-public mix that dominated the electric power business from 1907 on. Much—but not all—of what Insull wrought is what deregulation is meant to dismantle.

An Englishman by birth, Insull became Edison's assistant at age 21. As Edison's business manager, Insull mastered the minutiae of the utility world. He had the raw nerve to turn down an offer from Morgan, and soon emerged at the helm of Chicago's power business. But Insull was savvy enough to realize that baronial monopolies could not last forever. The profits were too huge and too visible. The abuses were too rampant. The grassroots surge toward public ownership was too strong.

Insull soon became president of the National Electric Light Association, formed in the 1880s as the infant industry's private front group. In 1898 he presented the NELA with what would become the underlying structure of the modern utility business. "The best service at the lowest possible price can only be obtained," he said, "by exclusive control of a given territory being placed in the hands of one undertaking." The "natural monopoly" of electric power demanded a publicly regulated network of privately owned monoliths. Each company's territory would be protected. Its return on investment would be virtually guaranteed. It would provide service to all those within the district who demanded it. In exchange, regulation would protect the monopolies from both private competition and outright public ownership.

In other words, "wasteful competition" would be abolished. A public-private partnership would run the show.

Some executives reacted with horror. But Insull's formula caught on, because the barons of electricity knew they could control the commissions meant to regulate them. Similar panels proliferated throughout U.S. industry, in railroads and food production, telecommunications and finance. In all cases the regulatory mode deflected public anger while offering the corporate chieftains an official way to protect and rationalize their empires. As Milwaukee Mayor Daniel Hoan put it in 1907, when electric regulatory commissions were established in Wisconsin and New York: "No shrewder piece of political humbuggery and downright fraud has ever been placed upon the statute books. It's supposed to be legislation for the people. In fact, it's legislation for the power oligarchy."

"What looks like a stone wall to a layman is a triumphal arch to a corporate lawyer," added the humorist Thomas Dooley.

As early as 1912, the Stone and Webster construction company (a future builder of nuclear power plants) owned the rights to two-thirds of the nation's water power. In 1916, Insull alone controlled 118 companies in nine states. By 1921 every state but Delaware had established a utility regulatory commission. By then the radical farm-labor movements of the new century had been crushed in the reactionary Red Scare that followed World War I. Rampant materialism roared over the 1920s.

In a conservative age, the states obliged the moneyed interests by crippling the spread of public power. More and more munis were forced to buy their juice from private producers. From 1923 to 1927 the U.S. lost more than a quarter of its 3,066 public power systems.

Meanwhile, the vaguely regulated monopolies were left free to swallow up other utilities. Holding companies and mega-trusts took the utility business into fewer and fewer hands. By the mid 1920s Insull and fifteen fellow Barons owned 85% of the nation's electricity supply. "Nothing like this gigantic monopoly has ever appeared in the history of the world," lamented Gifford Pinchot, two-time Republican Governor of Pennsylvania.

By 1929 the House of Morgan alone controlled more than a third of the nation's electricity supply. Insull accounted for another ten percent.

And then, with the autumn leaves, it all began to fall apart.

PART TWO: NUKING THE NEW DEAL

Chapter Three:
An Electric New Deal

High atop the booming utility juggernaut, Sam Insull spent the Roaring Twenties building himself a throne of gold. Electric power was the "can't miss" investment of the decade, the technological miracle whose stocks were snapped up as fast as their promoters could print the certificates. Insull was the era's business whiz. Everything he touched turned to gold. His January, 1929 issue of the Utility Investments Corporations jumped from $12 to $150 per share. According to one biographer, his $150 million personal worth grew at the rate of $7,000 per minute, 24 hours a day.

With 75% of the utility industry controlled by ten holding companies, stock issues soared beyond all reason. Insull's empire alone served four million customers and controlled $3 billion in assets. More than a half million people owned its stocks and bonds.

But like so many other big speculators, Insull thought the ride could never end. He borrowed and reborrowed against his real assets. The torrent of cash generated by his paper fortune bought still more pieces of the utility pie, against which he borrowed still more to finance still more speculation.

Even after the Crash of '29, Insull kept buying more generating plants and transmission lines, then using them to finance additional expansion. He'd already survived the Crash of 1893, just after J.P. Morgan pushed Tom Edison out of the electric business. And his Middle West Utilities Company served nearly five thousand communities in thirty states and Canada through 239 operating companies, two dozen holding companies and thirteen affiliated subsidiaries. Insull was president of eleven companies, chairman of sixty-five and a director of eighty-five. His titanic holdings might take a bump or two, but he was hardly alone in thinking them unsinkable.

Reality broke through on April 8, 1932. Utility stocks were finally plunging back toward something resembling the value of the real assets behind them. Insull was hopelessly overextended. The shrunken face value of his stocks could not sustain his huge debt. In the pinch of the endgame, he crawled to his ancient rival, the House of Morgan, which said no.

Nineteen separate Insull companies fell into bankruptcy. Stocks plunged across the board, wiping out between $500 million and $3 billion in paper capital. Ordinary working people everywhere saw their life savings obliterated. One utility stock dropped from $80 per share to 25 cents. Another plunged from $68.12 to $1.25. The collapse, said a Chicago banker, "hurt our city more than did the great fire."

Insull's demise ended an era. In early 1933, the National Electric Light Association, the industry front group Insull had helped build, quietly dissolved. It reformed as the Edison Electric Institute (which later became a leading booster of atomic energy). The shock wave of utility bankruptcies ruined millions of simple investors who'd staked everything on the limitless future of electric power. They'd been tragically misled to trust corporate minions riding the device of the holding company to vastly inflated public prices for overextended assets.

But they were right about the technology. From 1929 to 1933, residential use of electricity actually increased twenty percent. The spread of home appliances, office lighting and electrified mass transit boosted demand. While the speculative holding trusts plummeted into chaos, many of the actual operating companies still turned a profit. Philadelphia Electric, for example, paid a handsome dividend in 1932 even as utility speculators crashed all around it.

Ironically, the structure of regulated monopolies Insull had pioneered at the turn of the century stood the industry well in the Great Crash. While his holding companies collapsed, the business itself remained relatively stable. Once the speculative wreckage was cleared away, the actual business of producing and delivering electricity proved sound.

Especially in the public power districts. Their prices remained lower, their service more reliable and their finances more stable.

Their champion was U.S. Senator George W. Norris. Born dirt-poor on a backwater Ohio farm, Norris became a Nebraska attorney and then, in 1902, a Republican Congressman.

Norris and Insull agreed that utilities were a "natural monopoly." But while Insull cruised from riches to rags, Norris fought tirelessly to bring the electric power industry under direct public ownership.

In 1913, the state of California passed the Unjust Competition Act, banning private utilities from selling electricity at specially discounted rates designed to drive public power companies out of business. (Such predatory pricing is still around, and is key to the modern disaster of deregulation).

In 1920, Congress passed the Federal Water Power Act as a compromise in the public-private struggle over control of America's rivers. But enforcement was left to a part-time agency. The act was revised in 1930. But holding companies still controlled 85% of the country's electric generation, and routinely refused agency requests even for basic information.

Then came the crash of "the Insull Monstrosity," as New York Governor Franklin Delano Roosevelt bitterly denounced it. In their "destruction of local control" and "substitution of absentee management," FDR said, the holding companies had "built up in the public-utility field what has justly been called a system of private socialism which is inimical to the welfare of a free people." Backed by a revived farm-labor movement, FDR's 1933 New Deal Congress pledged to bring the private utilities to account, and to spread Norris's vision of public ownership.

As the New Deal took off, a conservative Supreme Court surprisingly pierced private power's legal fortress. "The due process clause of the Fourteenth Amendment," the Court ruled in 1933, "does not insure to public utilities the right under all circumstances to have a return upon the value of the property so used. The loss of, or the failure to obtain patronage, due to competition, does not justify the imposition of charges that are exorbitant and unjust to the public." The pro-business Supremes thus told the utility Barons it was not the government's job to protect them from "business hazards." The decision helped pave the way for New Deal reforms. Six decades later it gives the lie to the idea that utilities are somehow entitled to public compensation for bad investments.

On May 24, 1935, from the White House, FDR threw the switch for 20,000 fans at major league baseball's first night game, played at Cincinnati's Crosley Field (the Reds beat the Phillies, 2-1).

Meanwhile the Federal Power Act was updated to regulate wholesale contracts and limit utility executives from running other banks or utilities without permission. Unfortunately, in ensuing years, such permission was rarely denied.

Also in 1935, Congress passed the fiercely contested Public Utility Holding Company Act (PUHCA), meant to break up the paper empires through which the House of Morgan and other bankers and speculators still dominated electricity. But PUHCA left in tact nine big and some seventy smaller holding companies. It moderated the future growth of the utility empires. But it failed to break them.

Along with the Securities and Exchange Commission, the Federal Power Commission (later the Federal Electric Regulatory Commission) established national controls on the interstate electric power business, filling in where state regulators could not go. But New Deal legislation failed to break the private stranglehold over transmission lines. Specifically, it did not define them as public carriers, which would have forced their use as open highways carrying the power of rival generators. Thus the big private utilities could still surround and isolate public systems, a sixty-year death blow to the spread of real competition.

Nonetheless, in the wake of the New Deal, electric prices stabilized, as did the industry. There would be no further utility bankruptcies for a half-century (until the 1980s) when atomic reactors would take down the Public Service Company of New Hampshire and the Washington Public Power Supply System.

In the interim, grassroots outrage over Insull and the excesses of the electric barons pushed public power to the head of the parade. Senator Norris pressed his dream of bringing electricity to millions of rural households. Raised in agrarian destitution, Norris believed rural cooperatives could improve millions of lives by delivering electrons to pump water, light homes and barns and operate machinery.

The private power companies fought every inch of the way. But the 1936 Rural Electrification Act brought a new technological dawn to America's poorest farmers. Funding from the Public Works Administration helped push rural coops into the continent's farthest reaches. By 1944, nearly half America's farms had electric power. In the sweep of its vision and the scope of its success, the REA revolutionized American rural life in what Norris called "the spirit of unselfishness for the greatest good to the greatest number."

FDR and Norris also envisioned huge federal power districts, most importantly in the Tennessee and Columbia River Valleys, as well as along the St. Lawrence River and at Boulder (now Hoover) Dam. For flood control and irrigation, for cheap power and to circumvent the private monopolies, the New Dealers created the Tennessee Valley

Authority and Bonneville Power Authority, America's biggest public power districts.

For decades utility executives had branded government utilities as a form of "creeping socialism." But TVA and BPA were a flying leap. Norris had been fighting for years to base a public power district around a World War I power plant at Muscle Shoals, Alabama. FDR finally signed off on the new authority on May 18, 1933. In February, 1934, Director David Lilienthal signed TVA's first wholesale supply deal with Tupelo, Mississippi (where Elvis was about to be born). Soon the Alcorn County Electric Coop joined in. Over the next five years, voters defied ferocious utility campaigns and approved 62 of 72 public elections for membership in TVA. In 1938 the U.S. Supreme Court upheld TVA's mandate. Despite relentless opposition, by 1941 TVA operated 21 dams and provided 38 rural coops and 76 municipal utilities with rates far below those charged by the privates.

The northwest got cheap power from BPA's abundant Columbia River hydro. More than 740 rural coops came on-line through the REA. Sixty "public utility districts" were created in eighteen states. Norris's Nebraska got all its power through public suppliers. And farmers throughout the south, midwest and west held mock "funerals" for their newly obsolete kerosene lanterns, welcoming the age of electricity into the deepest pockets of rural poverty.

In 1940 FDR won an unprecedented third term by defeating Wendell Willkie, a utility mogul. At the brink of World War II, the march of municipal power seemed unstoppable.

Chapter Four:
The Nuclear Delusion

After the bombing of Hiroshima marked the end of World War II, Albert Einstein warned that the facts about atomic energy must be carried "to the village square." From there, he said, "must come America's voice."

That New Deal voice helped public-owned utilities to thrive and grow, even after FDR's death in 1945. "The Republicans don't like to sell cheap public power because it means the big power monopolies cannot get their rake-off at the expense of the public," said Harry Truman on the way to his surprise 1948 re-election.

In 1952, the last year of Truman's term, his Paley Commission outlined an American energy future built around the sun. There would be 15 million solar-heated homes in the United States by 1975, it said. Power would also come from natural sources such as windmills and photovoltaic cells, which convert sunlight directly to electricity. All of which could doom the large, centralized, privately-owned utilities..

But the 1952 election of Dwight Eisenhower short-circuited that vision. As television sets poured into

American living rooms, and private utilities pumped their sales with "all-electric homes" and a whole new world of miracle appliances, Ike inaugurated a nuclear-fueled attack on public power.

Under cover of Cold War McCarthyism, private utilities again assaulted muni advocates as "socialists and communists" out to destroy "the American system of government." As they had during the Red Scare after World War I, and through the Roaring Twenties, Congress and the states made it ever harder to establish new public power districts. The monopoly stranglehold over transmission lines was a major factor. But the atom was the ultimate guarantor of future private dominance.

The Bomb's obliteration of two whole cities horrified humankind. But its raw power provoked visions of what Atomic Energy Commission Chairman Glenn Seaborg called "a new world through nuclear technology." "Planetary engineering" would spawn legions of reactors, each with "its own little Eden." Mass media brimmed with delusions of nuke-powered aircraft, SCUBA gear and wrist watches. Homes built with uranium ore would generate their own power. Whole cities would radiate heat to melt snow before it fell. Alvin Weinberg, who patented the water-cooled nuclear reactor, epitomized the culture when he described himself as an "Ayatollah" about this "inexhaustible energy source." In September, 1954, Lewis Strauss, a close Eisenhower advisor and another AEC Chairman, made the ultimate vow: "It is not too much to expect that our children will enjoy in their homes electrical energy too cheap to meter."

In a special 1953 United Nations address, Ike promised the world the infinite benefits of "Atoms for Peace."

But despite the hype, nuclear power was still mostly about the Bomb. In a secret 1946 report, Under Secretary of State Dean Acheson, and Atomic Energy Commission Chairman David Lilienthal, made it clear: "The development of atomic energy for peaceful purposes and the development of atomic energy for bombs are in much of their course interchangeable and interdependent."

After all, the AEC employed tens of thousands of people at scores of multi-billion-dollar facilities. A civilian industry could expand the AEC empire and paint a happy face on a technology that threatened the world. Remote, capital-intensive, high-tech and usable only for centralized systems, it was the perfect antidote to solar power.

With the 1954 Atomic Energy Act, Congress authorized the AEC to both promote the new technology and regulate its safety. But key scientists believed commercial reactors were dangerous and impractical. The utilities agreed. Said *Business Week*: "You can find a great many more buyers for the Brooklyn Bridge than businessmen interested in doing something about atomic power."

So the AEC and the military pitched in with basic research—to the ultimate tune of more than $100 billion. Working with Westinghouse, the Navy's Admiral Hyman Rickover built the nuclear-powered Nautilus submarine. The first dedicated commercial reactor, was built at Shippingport, near Westinghouse's Pittsburgh headquarters. Mimicking FDR, Ike touched off its construction by remote control. But the outcome was infinitely more menacing than night baseball.

Westinghouse and the other nuke promoters dubbed their reactors "inherently safe." But a secret Brookhaven National Laboratory report showed an accident at Shippingport or another commercial plant could immediately kill 3,400 people, injure another 43,000 and irradiate 150,000 square miles (an area "the size of Pennsylvania") doing at least $7 billion damage. The AEC's own Advisory Committee on Reactor Safety warned that the security of reactors in populated areas had "not been established experimentally, and must be so before the operation of a reactor could possibly be recommended." Utility and insurance companies balked at the risk.

So in 1957 Congress passed the Price-Anderson Act. A $540 million federal fund would cap civilian claims from a reactor catastrophe. The utilities would be exempt from lawsuits. Individual victims would be out of luck.

By then the United Auto Workers were fighting Detroit Edison's "fast breeder" reactor in Monroe, south of Detroit. AEC Commissioner Strauss termed the union's resistance "the first indications that the private development of atomic power would be fought." He argued the safety issues raised by the UAW and its lead attorney, an MIT-trained engineer named Leo Goodman, would be answered once the reactor opened. U.S. Supreme Court Justice William O. Douglas called that "a lighthearted approach to the most awesome, the most deadly, the most dangerous process that man has ever created." But only Justice Hugo Black voted with him. By 7-2, the Supremes let Fermi fire up. In 1966, it melted, as lamented by John G. Fuller in the aptly titled *We Almost Lost Detroit*.

Despite tens of billions of dollars in federal subsidies for research, development, fuel production, waste disposal, insurance and more, private utility executives were squeamish. So the nuke pushers turned to public power. After the New Deal, the Bonneville Power

Authority and Tennessee Valley Authority became large, unwieldy bureaucracies, run by increasingly conservative Washington appointees, ever more removed from their constituent-customers. With their massive coal burners and other environmentally sensitive projects, the federal power authorities became some of the nation's worst polluters.

TVA also hosted the massive national nuclear laboratory at Oak Ridge, Tennessee. BPA served the Hanford weapons facility in the deserts of eastern Washington. So as "free market" zealots demanded the huge federal combines be sold to pay off the national debt, public power gave the private nuke industry a critical boost. Pushed in part by Democratic Senator Al Gore, Sr., of Tennessee, TVA and BPA together contracted for more reactors than any other single U.S. buyer except Commonwealth Edison of Chicago. Other public power districts and rural coops also bought in. Though dominated by public power companies, Nebraska hosted a nuke. So did the Sacramento Municipal Utility District. Even Students for a Democratic Society, the radical campus crusade, cited atomic energy as a potential solution to the plight of the world's poor in its founding statement.

In the early 1960s, John Kennedy announced that some 95% of the nation's farms now had electricity. A New Deal dream had been fulfilled.

But as the Vietnam War began killing other dreams, New Yorkers worried about safety stopped a reactor in the borough of Queens. Cost-conscious voters in Eugene killed a project slated for Pebble Springs, Oregon. Northern Californians turned a project at quake-prone Bodega Head into just an empty crater.

Nonetheless, by the early 1970s, a national consensus around the dream of the Peaceful Atom seemed secure. The reactor rush turned slap-dash. "The average utility knew as much about the nuclear plant it was buying as the average car-buyer knows about cars," said one executive. "They knew how big it was, and what it cost. We got into nuclear power because the president of my utility used to play golf with the president of another utility. They bought one, and so we bought one."

But state regulators often set investment returns based on how much money utilities had sunk into their physical plant. The more they spent, the more profit they could gross. And nothing could guarantee a booming cash flow or escalate a bottom line better than a hugely expensive nuclear construction project.

In the wake of the Arab oil embargo, Dick Nixon promised a thousand U.S. reactors by the year 2000. As he spoke in 1974, there were 236 on line, under construction or on order. The overall investment was hurtling toward a half-trillion dollars. (Nixon also predicted "a completely new restructuring of the industry" by century's end, with the nation's electricity controlled by "only 15 to 20" super utilities).

As the Peaceful Atom became the centerpiece of the American utility system, the industry remained firmly in private hands. Almost without exception, munis provided electricity more cheaply than the privates (now known as "Investor Owned Utilities"—IOUs). But just ten percent of the nation's electric power came from federal agencies like TVA and BPA. The percentage coming from small municipals, which was at 7% in 1933, rose to just 9% into the 1980s. More than half the electricity that flowed through the rural coops was coming from private sources.

Under Eisenhower, the restrictions on consolidation of utility ownership laid down in the 1935 Public Utility Holding Company Act were relaxed. Huge power pools now linked the nation's suppliers into the semblance of a national grid. The oligopoly dwarfed the fondest dreams of Morgan and Insull. Some 85% of the nation's electricity flowed through the wires of just 17 consortiums. The revolving door between regulatory commissions, utility boardrooms and nuke builders spun like a turbine.

The U.S. utility industry was among the world's very largest businesses in terms of both annual sales and invested capital. With its future planning built around the Peaceful Atom, it approached the new millennium secure in its regulatory cocoon.

Or so it seemed.

technologies deep in the background. But the human and ecological price has been astronomical. To begin with, our centralized system wastes some seventy percent of the energy inherent in the fossil fuels it burns. In tandem with auto emissions, utility coal and oil burners remain the nation's worst source of air pollution in myriad forms—from particulate emissions and acid rain to ozone depletion and greenhouse gases. Thousands die annually from asthma, lung cancer and other utility-related diseases. The social and medical costs are incalculable, and are escalating. From oil spills and well fires to toxic runoff and strip mining, from dead lakes and lethal smog to mountaintop removal and deforestation the soaring costs of mining, processing and burning fossil fuels have been among the great plagues of human existence. Massive hydro-electric dams, once thought to be relatively benign, have also wreaked havoc with the natural environment. Rarely does the "market economy" account for the health, ecological and aesthetic costs that are so vital to human existence. But clearly, humankind is to survive, other ways of generating power must be used.

By publicizing the health dangers of DDT, Rachel Carson's 1962 *Silent Spring* helped arouse a new ecological consciousness. By 1970 growing public concern sparked the first national Earth Day. Amidst the agony of the Vietnam fiasco, President Nixon termed the environment "the issue of the decade." Congress passed the Environmental Protection, Clean Air and Clean Water Acts. All would mandate curbs on the poisons with which utilities showered the countryside.

By 1976, amidst the rise of a national anti-nuclear movement, Amory Lovins and Barry Commoner laid out revolutionary blueprints. Lovins's "Road Not Taken" (published in *Foreign Affairs Magazine*) charted a "soft energy path" toward efficiency and renewables. Commoner's *Politics of Energy* and other writings showed that natural gas, eventually produced organically, could be the bridge to a solar future. Fossil fuels and nuclear power would soon be obsolete.

The technologies on which Lovins and Commoner built their visions were publicly scorned by the IOUs and their toadies. But as outlined in Ray Reece's 1979 *Sun Betrayed*, the fossil-nuke industries did the traditional Robber Baron thing through the "corporate seizure of U.S. solar energy development." In short, they monopolized and suppressed key breakthroughs in renewable and efficiency technologies while loudly trashing their potential. Reactionary and complacent architectural and home building industries aborted the 15 million solar-heated homes promised by the Paley Commission a quarter-century earlier. Fossil fuels stayed cheap, thanks largely to numerous military interventions in oil-producing nations. The multinationals that controlled those fuels, and the utilities that burned them, wanted to sell more electricity, not less.

The 1976 election of Jimmy Carter dented the prevailing mindset. Declaring "the moral equivalent of war," Carter donned a sweater, stuck a solar water heater on the White House roof, and talked about burning less imported fossil fuel. He emphasized, among other things, that the U.S. wastes fully half the energy it consumes, and that merely increasing our efficiency could go a very long way toward saving our planet.

In 1978 Congress passed the Public Utility Regulatory Policies Act (PURPA), forcing utilities to buy power funded photovoltaics' early growth spurt. But Reagan-Bush (1981-1993) decimated anything meant to boost renewables. Reagan tore Carter's solar water heater off the White House roof and killed nearly all clean energy research. Bush proclaimed himself "a President of the United States that came out of the oil and gas industry, that knows it and knows it well."

A preoccupied Clinton Administration (with a chief advisor, Mac MacLarty, from the gas industry) failed to pick up the solar slack. The most promising patents and producers have been bought up by German, Japanese and Israeli firms. Their businesses are booming, particularly in developing nations, some of which may seek to avoid or minimize their dependence on the kinds of central grid systems now proving so unwieldy in the developed world. At some point in the new century, the world's electric supply could very well center around photovoltaics. But American industry may be left in the shadows.

Ditto wind power. When the Paley Commission reported, blades still turned everywhere on American farms, pumping water and providing basic power. Subsidized fossil fuels sent most of them to the scrap heap.

But with centuries of experience, Denmark has turned modern techniques to the wind. Their biggest early customer was California. When Jerry Brown became governor in 1975, he brought in a progressive young PUC Commissioner named John Bryson. Special tax credits and other programs sparked the siting of some 15,000 windmills, which produced enough power to light San Francisco. The U.S. was the world's leader in wind-driven electricity. Massive wind resources, especially between the Rockies and the Mississippi, could still make the U.S. "the Saudi Arabia of wind." By early 1999, prices for wind-driven electricity were down to 4-5 cents/kilowatt-hour, easily cheap enough to undercut nuclear power and compete with coal and oil.

But Reagan-Bush had crippled the U.S. research and development structure. When Republican George Deukmejian succeeded Brown in 1983, he did the same to California's tax credits. Danish domination of global manufacturing and design advanced. In the late 1990s, Germany took the lead in kilowatt hours produced by the wind. Despite the U.S. retreat, wind power has become the fastest-growing new source of electric generation worldwide.

And there are other technologies. Based on hydrogen, fuel cells (also boosted by the space program) offer a clean, compact, cheapening power source that can move vehicles and heat and light houses.

Hydrogen may be the mobile fuel of the new millennium. It can be produced by zapping water with solar electricity. When "burned," hydrogen's only by-product is the water from which it was extracted. But hydrogen is versatile enough to power vehicles and heat large structures, in rapidly advancing fuel cells and by other means. As a clean and cheap fuel, hydrogen's future appears unlimited.

Likewise solar thermal plants. They can focus solar rays on tubes or tanks, boiling liquids to create steam. A power tower and an array of solar collectors thrived in the California deserts until hostile state and federal policies spelled their financial doom. Ocean thermal techniques, which turn temperature differentials into power, also wait in the wings.

Meanwhile, fickle federal policies have stalked farm-based biomass (plant products) meant for usable energy.

Burning crops and plant residues directly has long been posited as a potential for renewable energy supplies. More attractive has been fermenting corn, sugar beets, bagasse (sugar cane remnants) and other organic matter into ethanol and methane. Through the 1980s and '90s farm and food processing interests—led by the multi-national Archer, Daniels Midland—kept subsidies in place for ethanol, used as a supplement to gasoline, among other things.

But the key "transition fuel" remains methane (natural gas) the major driving force behind utility deregulation. Along with dropping 1990s prices came major advances that drove down costs while allowing gas-fired generators of all shapes and sizes to be built quickly and cheaply. Combined cycle technology (co-generation) lets a single burner produce both heat and electricity at one site. With their need to guarantee a sure power supply at all times no matter what happens to the central grid, hospitals were among the first to adopt co-gen. But along with fuel cells, co-gen is already a strong alternative for factories, office buildings and other big users hoping to achieve for themselves more energy independence than Nixon or Carter won for the nation.

Unfortunately, natural gas can be a powerful contributor to global warming. Its mining and transport can also have severe environmental impacts. And its low price levels may not last.

So the long-term key to the ecologically sound use of methane is in its production by biological means, for which Commoner has long argued. In the interim, natural gas has gotten a wide green embrace as a "least worst" alternative, a relatively clean, readily available answer to gasoline in transportation, and to coal and oil in large generating plants and home heating.

Methane and fuel cells now threaten the utilities' future by offering their core customers a way to generate their own power (as did J.P. Morgan in his Fifth Avenue mansion). They can think about getting off the grid, or even pumping juice back into it. They could decimate the private utility industry, and open up that long-deferred bridge to an energy future based on the sun and wind.

But the radioactive corpse of the atomic mistake still blocks the soft path not yet taken.

Chapter Six:
No More Nukes

Despite the hype, the Peaceful Atom bred plenty of scientific skepticism. Manhattan Project leader Robert Oppenheimer and AEC Chair David Lilienthal both felt commercial atomic power might fail. Edward Teller, self-proclaimed father of the H-Bomb, warned that catastrophic accidents were virtually inevitable—and acceptable.

The anti-Fermi United Auto Worker lawsuit and early rebellions in New York, Oregon and California were underlined by massive grid failures that blacked out the Northeast and elsewhere. A certain public insecurity arose.

With the Vietnam war still raging, a top AEC medical researcher, Dr. John Gofman, warned that radioactive emissions from commercial reactors might be killing 32,000 Americans a year. For refusing to fudge or bury his data, the AEC forced Gofman out.

Meanwhile, University of Pittsburgh physicist Ernest Sternglass charged that the nearby Shippingport plant threatened the area's health. Like every other scientist who dared contradict the atomic industry, he and Gofman were ostracized as "non-credible" mavericks. But along with a courageous stream of fellow whistleblowers, Gofman and Sternglass spent the next three decades warning that nuclear energy could be lethal. They were joined in the early seventies by consumer advocate Ralph Nader, who warned the public that if they know the truth about atomic power, they'd opt for candles to light their homes. In 1974 and 1975 Nader hosted the first national "Critical Mass" activist gatherings on atomic power.

Meanwhile the word spread to proposed rural reactor sites like Montague, Massachusetts; Black Fox, Oklahoma; Tyrone, Wisconsin and San Luis Obispo. Vietnam-era activists often joined conservative locals to build a non-violent mass movement at the cutting green edge. The reactors were unsafe, ecologically destructive, and economically suicidal. Put the money into solar energy and efficiency, we argued, or eventually the IOUs would stick the public with a very big bill.

In 1975, $100 million came due when a TVA reactor at Browns Ferry, Alabama, was set afire by an inspector using a lighted candle.

A year later the U.S. Supreme Court ruled that limiting donations to election campaigns violated the First Amendment. In their infamous 1976 *Buckley v Vallejo* decision, the Justices equated free speech with the practice of pouring money into campaign coffers and thus buying (or renting) elected officials. No decision has proved a greater barrier to saving the environment or winning a solar future. It's forced green activists to constantly face state and national legislators who owe their jobs to the big polluters, with the IOUs at the head of the parade. And it's guaranteed that when citizens turn to referenda, they are massively outspent.

Thus in 1976, as Lovins and Commoner published

their solar manifestoes, anti-nuclear initiatives were buried in six states under an avalanche of IOU slush money. Yet reactor builders never submitted a single specific construction project to a popular vote, and rode roughshod over local opposition everywhere.

Including Seabrook, New Hampshire. After the town resolved four times against the two reactors proposed there, mass demonstrations erupted. On April 30, 1977, 1414 demonstrators were dragged off the site. More than 500 were then locked in National Guard armories for two media saturated weeks. Worldwide coverage helped spark mass arrests at Diablo Canyon, New York's Shoreham, Three Mile Island, and elsewhere. On June 24, 1978, twenty thousand packed a peaceful rally at Seabrook. Thousands more demonstrated that summer at other reactors around the U.S., and in Europe and Japan. The No Nukes network had gone global.

The following spring, Jane Fonda and Michael Douglas released a fictional feature about a reactor meltdown called *The China Syndrome*. Eerily, on March 28, a hydrogen bubble threatened to shatter Pennsylvania's Three Mile Island in a real-life drama that played like the film. While industry flaks denied it was happening, virtually all the fuel inside TMI-2's containment turned to molten radioactive metal. The entire northeast hung at the brink of an unfathomable catastrophe. No one will ever know precisely how much radiation poured out of the plant or where it went. But hundreds of area residents were poisoned. Twenty years later, they were still being denied a jury trial for their damages.

TMI was the "Tet offensive of nuclear power." It definitively ended America's romance with the Peaceful Atom. Before it, a majority favored building new reactors; since, a majority has been opposed. Six weeks after the meltdown, 125,000 nuclear opponents marched on the Capitol in Washington. That fall, 200,000 packed Manhattan's Battery Park City. "No Nukes" became a mainstream conviction.

The trickle of cancellations that began with the Arab oil embargo became a flood. All reactors ordered after 1973 were eventually scrapped. Regulators were swamped by an aroused public fearful about safety and livid over the astronomical escalation of construction costs. In TMI's wake, regulators demanded hundreds of design, construction and operational changes. But the industry resisted, and very few were ever put into place.

Nonetheless, reactors originally projected to cost in the hundreds of millions soared into the billions, mostly due to dishonest forecasts, utility incompetence and mass theft on the construction sites. Originally hyped at under a billion dollars for two reactors, Seabrook soared to $6 billion for one. Long Island's Shoreham jumped to $7 billion. Diablo Canyon, Ohio's Perry, Com Ed's Byron and LaSalle all put regulators in the untenable position of adding into the rate base (and thus to ratepayer bills) gargantuan sums of money to finish reactors the public had never voted on and now did not want.

In 1983, the three counties surrounding Three Mile Island voted 3-1 against reopening Unit One there. But Ronald Reagan forced it back on line, commenting that this was not an issue on which the public should vote.

In February, 1985, while the battle still raged over Diablo Canyon, *Forbes Magazine* deemed nuclear power "a disaster on a monumental scale." *Forbes* put the Peaceful Atom's price tag in the range of a quarter-trillion, and said "only the blind, or the biased, can now think most of the money has been well spent."

At Perry, a January 31, 1986 earthquake damaged the reactor as well as nearby roads and bridges. Then Chernobyl exploded on April 26, spreading its radioactive poisons worldwide. Ohio Governor Richard Celeste asked Cleveland Electric Illuminating to delay opening Perry until the state could re-study its evacuation planning. CEI refused. Ohio sued. Perry went critical only after a federal court denied the state jurisdiction.

But a second unit at Perry—already under construction—was forced down. So was Seabrook II, Indiana's Bailly and Marble Hill and the virtually complete Zimmer, near Cincinnati. Hundreds of millions of dollars were written off as pure waste, tabs the utility companies are always happy to pass on to the public—and to now count as "stranded costs."

Soon fully licensed, operating, hugely expensive reactors were being forced shut—six of them between 1989 and 1992. At Rowe, Massachusetts; Trojan, Oregon; Ft. St. Vrain in Colorado and California's San Onofre One, obsolete, inefficient reactors closed down. On Long Island, public outrage over cost and evacuation planning killed the $7 billion Shoreham reactor after a single 5% test run.

And in Sacramento, a June 1989 referendum shut the Rancho Seco reactor, the first such public vote. Because the plant was owned by the Sacramento Municipal Utility District, the vote was definitive. As the reactor shut, solar panels installed alongside it continued to produce electricity.

SMUD hired former TVA chief S. David Freeman to replace Rancho Seco's capacity with a conversion program built around solar, wind and increased efficiency. A half-million shade trees—"air conditioners with leaves"—were planted to cut summer electricity consumption. Trade-outs on inefficient refrigerators were subsidized. Photovoltaics, solar water heaters and wind farms were added to the mix. The program, boasted Freeman, proceeded "ahead of schedule and under budget." A single rate hike to fund the Rancho Seco shutdown was followed by a decade of rate stability.

With SMUD as a model, the grassroots dream of a post-nuclear energy economy built around renewables and efficiency lurched toward reality.

In 1992 economist Charles Komanoff calculated the bill for construction, research, development and other costs related to U.S. atomic power through 1990: $492 billion, accruing at the rate of some $50 billion/year. This did not include the potential costs for future accidents, or unexpected environmental and other damages for future waste management, or health damage from emissions exposures or other intangibles. The kilo-watt/hour costs of nuclear-generated electricity, Komanoff wrote, were far above those of fossil fuels; renewables were, at very least, cost competitive, and bound to get even cheaper. And increased efficiency was the most cost effective of all.

Komanoff's calculations were underlined by spectacular financial meltdowns at Seabrook and multiple reactor projects in the Washington Public Power Supply System (WHOOPS!). Major U.S. utilities fell into their first bankruptcies since Sam Insull's 1932 collapse. Shutdowns and phase-outs continued through the 1990s. Then the Clinton Administration finally erased the mythical divide between civilian and military technology by agreeing to use a TVA reactor to generate tritium gas for hydrogen bombs.

Despite all that, in early 1999 the Nuclear Regulatory Commission approved plans for a new generation of commercial reactors. Smaller and simpler than previous models, Westinghouse hoped its AB600 would revive the business it had begun with government subsidies four decades earlier at Shippingport. As with the previous generation, Westinghouse dubbed its new design "inherently safe."

But Three Mile Island, Chernobyl and the financial disaster that is atomic energy guarantees that future reactor construction will meet ferocious opposition. In Germany, Sweden, Italy, Austria and the rest of Europe, the experiment has been abandoned. Even the "model" French industry has declared a moratorium on new construction. The last likely major reactor markets, China and India, are shaky at best.

There, the universal core issues of health, safety, waste management, economics and home rule remain in bitter dispute. The rapid advance of solar, wind, efficiency and co-generation are pushing atomic power into the economic and ecological waste bin. By mid-1999, the number of U.S. reactors on line was down from a peak of around 112 to just 104. Dozens of aging plants still teeter on the brink, with parallel declines worldwide.

Had the U.S. taken the solar route prescribed in Harry Truman's 1952 Paley Report, the world's energy economy would be on a stable, ecologically sound footing. Wars for oil would be a thing of the past. All of us would be significantly richer, materially, ecologically, and in terms of our health.

But as it is, the Peaceful Atom's ubiquitous mark is

that of the most expensive technological failure in human history. Its uniquely destructive radioactive legacies will plague the planet for generations to come.

And now its perpetrators want to make you pay for it.

PART FOUR: AN ELECTRIC MILLENNIUM

Chapter Seven:
The Empire Strikes Back

At the dawn of the new millennium the IOU empire pioneered by Brush and Edison, Morgan and Insull, stands as a mighty fortress, about to transform itself.

Despite 120 years of campaigning, public power accounts for less than one-fifth of America's electricity. Half of that comes from TVA, BPA and other federal power districts. Most of the rest comes from municipals and rural coops, many of which merely redistribute IOU-generated electrons.

But public power remains a constant threat to private utilities. In the late 1970s, as the anti-nuke movement hit its stride, Cleveland Electric Illuminating tried to strongarm Dennis Kucinich into abolishing Muni Light. When "the boy mayor" evoked the populist resistance of Tom Johnson, Cleveland's financial elite black-mailed the city. A bought media smeared Kucinich. But two decades later, CEI's nuke-laden rates soared far beyond Muni Light's. Hailed a hero, Kucinich was elected to Congress in 1996. Re-elected in 1998, he has pioneered legislation meant to democratize and clean up the electric power business.

Through the 1980s and '90s, safe energy activists moved a parallel vision, hammering at state public utilities commissions to reshape the IOUs. "The agenda has been simple," says Wenonah Hauter of Ralph Nader's Critical Mass Energy Project. "We want to do for consumers and the planet what the market won't."

The atom's political and economic fallout weakened IOU dominance. In state after state they faced ferocious battles over their failing nuke investments.

Meanwhile, Lovins and others pushed "demand side management." DSM promoted energy efficiency by rewarding utilities for reducing demand and avoiding new plant construction. IOUs found themselves trying to reduce rather than expand the amount of power they sold. Some began marketing compact fluorescent light bulbs, energy-efficient refrigerators and other conservation devices. Through PURPA and state-by-state campaigning, activists forced wind and solar into the mix.

In a society that continues to waste at least half the fuel it burns, increased efficiency remains the cheapest and cleanest way to improve our energy future. But while individual efforts at increased efficiency can and will have enormous impact, the long-term effects of utility-based DSM were marginal. With deregulation, the efforts have deteriorated. As activists Dan Berman and John O'Connor put it, utilities would "not support a strategy that 'unsells' their main product."

Meanwhile, the plummeting price of natural gas and advances in renewables, co-generation and fuel cells struck at the core of the whole IOU domain. Studies by the Union of Concerned Scientists and others showed the U.S. could massively expand solar applications and gain both substantial savings and huge employment benefits. If big factories and office buildings did use methane and the sun to produce their own power cheaper than the utilities could deliver it, and even send it back into the grid, where's the future of the IOU?

In short, the utilities were trapped between a shrinking customer base, their huge nuke debts, and pro-solar activists still determined to shut reactors at their builders' expense.

As Sam Insull had pushed regulation to avoid public power, and as atomic energy had short-circuited solar power, the IOUs now had to escape the post-nuclear/cheap methane vice.

Their answer: deregulation.

In California, with help from some big industrial users, Enron jumped first. The huge Houston-based natural gas distributor thought its methane could dominate open electric markets, especially California's. The big users would co-generate. Stand-alone gas burners built by independents would flood the grid with cheap power. The fossil-nuke IOUs would be busted. As Barry Commoner had predicted, methane would usher in a new millennium.

But Enron failed to account for the "Darth Vader of utility deregulation." As a young Yale Law graduate, John Bryson had helped found the Natural Resources Defense Council, a pioneering environmental law firm. Then Jerry Brown made him chair of California's PUC, hoping for a new age of wind and solar power. When he became a Vice President of Southern California Edison, it was widely assumed Bryson would show that even a nuclear utility could push hard for renewables and efficiency.

But somewhere along the way, the Dark Side won out. Bryson emerged in 1990 as SoCalEd's President, with a million-plus annual salary, and a plan to keep San Onofre and Diablo Canyon on line—and solar energy at bay. He then led the charge for deregulation, inheriting Sam Insull's mantle at a transformative moment.

Bryson's manifesto became Assembly Bill 1890, drafted and presented to the legislature by Ann Cohn, Senior Legal Counsel for Bryson's Southern California Edison. Hyped at its 1996 introduction as the vehicle to open the state's giant market to competition, the bill was a wish list for IOUs stuck with big nukes. Immensely complex in its detail, AB1890's executive summary in essence read like this:

➤ Unload on the public bad reactor and other failed investments, including obsolete fossil burners;

➤ Grab huge sums of cash;

➤ Turn back public power;

➤ Co-opt and avoid green/consumer activism;

➤ Pre-empt big industrial co-generation;

➤ Cripple solar and efficiency;

➤ De-unionize.

First and foremost, AB1890 allowed California's IOUs a staggering $28.5 billion in "stranded costs." This now-infamous euphemism refers to the uncompensated capital sunk in generating facilities—mostly nuclear, coal or oil burners—that can't compete.

The IOU argument goes like this: since the PUC let these bum facilities into the rate base, the public should pay for "stranding" them. Forcing them to compete with cheaper, cleaner sources would be a "taking" of private property.

Stranded costs are the 800 pound gorilla of deregulation. San Diego Gas & Electric and Bryson's SoCalEd have two reactors at San Onofre. PG&E has the two at Diablo. Together they demanded a staggering ransom—

well over $10 billion, by some estimates as much as $14.5 billion—just to bail out those four nukes. Their plan was to turn the biggest failed investments in California history into gigantic liquid assets. The bitterly disputed Diablo Canyon cost overruns would be magically transformed into a source of ready cash.

Nationwide, Bryson's fellow IOU honchoes looked for a "stranded reactor" bailout estimated by the Safe Energy Communication Council's *Great Ratepayer Robbery* at somewhere between $120 and $200 billion. "This constitutes the largest single consumer rip-off in the history of the United States," says SECC Executive Director Scott Denman. "Ultimately, this theft could dwarf even the S&L bailout, which cost taxpayers $132 billion."

Legal precedent was against this shameless scam. The 1933 U.S. Supreme Court demanded the utilities face their own "business hazards." Similar opinions have followed from Judge Kenneth Starr, Rep. Dick Armey, the Cato Institute, the Heritage Foundation, the Wall Street Journal and a host of others, right, left and center (see Appendix).

But Bryson and the IOUs knew they could buy and bully the California PUC and legislature. They cut their first deal with the big industrials, who helped start the ball rolling. In the ultimate act of predatory pricing, they promised the factories and office buildings a rate cheap enough to undercut the tide of natural gas co-generation (stranding Enron). They would then make up the difference by jacking up rates for small businesses, homeowners and renters.

Meanwhile the IOUs took their stranded cost cash bonanza through "transition fees" and other surcharges buried in the fine print of the average utility bill.

For "competition," the transmission lines so carefully monopolized by the utilities for a century, would remain monopoly owned. But they would now serve as the open highways they should have been all along. Both quality of service and rate of return on those lines would still be regulated. But anyone could ship power over them. The customer could finally choose a supplier.

But not as a group. The hundred-year war between the IOUs and public power still raged, and the privates were not about to yield their upper hand. After all, Sacramento had voted shut a reactor in 1989, and was cheaply and quickly converting to precisely those green, decentralized sources that struck terror in the balance sheets of IOU bean counters.

So AB1890 encouraged industrial users to pool their demand and get cheaper rates from the grid. But it strictly limited the ability of individual citizens and communities to do the same. The city of San Francisco, for example, could not vote to buy power as a unit. Nor could its neighborhoods. Instead, any government wishing to "aggregate" its demand would have to laboriously— almost impossibly—collect individual signatures. If at all, the '90s version of public power would enter through the back door, hamstrung from the start.

Overall, the core of the dereg deal was simple: the utilities got a huge cash windfall, the big users got subsidized rates the utilities hoped would pre-empt industrial co-generation, and the small consumers' right to buy collectively was all but denied.

To top things off, the utilities took the privilege of reselling the names of their customers to private marketers, a stunning invasion of privacy. And they got the legislature to blow $90 million in public money to promote the very screwing that would cost the public another $28.5 billion!

As would be expected in a welfare scam this large, the utilities lavished the Public Utilities Commissioners and legislators with all the requisite junkets, campaign donations and ancillary perks. To sell AB1890 to the public, the IOUs hyped a 10% "discount," with rates frozen for five years. They promised that once the nukes were all paid off, competition would drive prices lower. But as consumer advocate Harvey Rosenfield put it, "they failed to explain that the rate cut was financed with a bond issue costing ratepayers far more in the long term than they thought they'd gained from the initial discount."

For all this, the industrial-utility alliance feared serious heat from California's powerful green consumer groups. So they trotted out Ralph Cavanagh.

Lead utility campaigner for NRDC, Cavanagh is a disciple of John Bryson. Using NRDC's green cover, Cavanagh made sure Bryson's bailout bill contained a few eco-scraps, including some money for efficiency and renewables. As Dan Berman and John O'Connor wrote in *Who Owns the Sun*, NRDC's huge budgets, with substantial money from the Energy Foundation, funded Cavanagh's ability to protect Bryson and sell AB1890 behind the scenes and in the media. "The Energy Foundation launders utility influence through the foundation system," says an activist who chooses to remain unidentified. "Under that cover, they use NRDC and their fellow high-rollers to buy green credibility for utility bailouts, while starving the grassroots organizations that really speak for the public."

Much of California's consumer-environmental community was (and still is) outraged. Energy experts such as Eugene Coyle, Nancy Rader and Paul Fenn bitterly objected that AB1890 prolonged operations at Diablo and San Onofre, gouged consumers, delayed renewables and gutted efficiency. "Electricity prices were poised to plummet due to technological advances and low gas prices," said Coyle. "Despite the 10% `discount,' AB1890 actually kept rates higher than they would have been with the onset of true competition."

Coyle added that the renewables subsidies touted by Cavanagh would probably expire before they could materialize. "They weren't needed anyway," he said. "Methane and wind were poised to transform California's energy economy before AB1890 stopped the transition."

But Cavanagh dominated the scant public debate around the biggest bailout in California history. Hearings were perfunctory and mostly ignored by the media. Badgered, bullied and bought by the state's biggest utilities and industrial users, the legislature passed the bill unanimously. Gov. Pete Wilson quickly signed it. Launched from America's biggest market, utility deregulation suddenly had all the momentum of a runaway reactor.

It quickly realized its opponents' worst fears. A year after enactment, less than one percent of California's consumers had switched to a new provider. Real competition was non-existent. Stranded cost "transition charges" made it impossible for new entrants to contend. Even the rich and powerful Enron had to bow out. Wind, solar and efficiency were driven into reverse both by the surcharges and by the general instability in energy investing. Industrial co-generation was (temporarily) frozen by heavily subsidized IOU electricity. SMUD was under attack from predatory PG&E pricing. Filthy old fossil burners, grandfathered from the Clean Air Act, continued to pump out pollutants.

Meanwhile Bryson joined PG&E and SDG&E in spending their huge stranded cost windfalls like drunken sailors. "They've transformed themselves into the `Amazon. coms' of energy," said Herb Gunther of San Francisco's Public Media Center. "They're spending on everything except the ratepayers of California."

Transforming SoCalEd into Edison International and Mission Energy, Bryson directed mega-sums of new investment capital into bitterly contested fossil burners in Mexico and throughout Asia. Bryson's dubious dealings with Indonesia's brutal Suharto regime, involving hundreds of millions of dollars, raised eyebrows with the Wall Street Journal and international regulators and jurists. Meanwhile, PG&E bought generators throughout the American east, gobbling up local dams and water rights along the way.

The promise of huge chunks of what Gunther called "rogue cash" thrilled IOUs everywhere. In Illinois (with a dozen badly performing nuclear plants), Pennsylvania (with 8), Michigan (5), Virginia (4), New Jersey (3) and other big states, dereg bills flew through pliant legislatures as fast as deals could be cut, junkets flown, and campaign contribution checks signed and delivered. A score of states handed fresh billions to the Robber Baron heirs of Insull and Westinghouse. Community choice was blocked through complex, virtually insurmountable legal strictures. Renewables and efficiency were frozen, consumer privacy compromised, nukes funded, lethal old fossil burners cranked to the hilt. With more than 500 filthy old coal plants exempted from the Clean Air Act, and with more than half the nation's electricity still coming from coal, the U.S. Public Interest Research Group warned that deregulation could help as much as triple certain forms of air pollution.

Congressional moves came rapidly to repeal PUHCA and end PURPA-enforced contracts for clean energy. The IOUs openly scorn efficiency and are again trying to sell as much electricity as possible, despite its escalating environmental impact. AB1890 wannabes have flooded Congress and the states, with Cavanagh running eager interference. In a wave of mega-mergers, the IOUs skirt or merely ignore PUHCA. A network of unregulated monopolies—the "15-20 super utilities" predicted by Nixon—is replacing the regulated one Insull established nine decades ago.

Not only have the utilities (so far) escaped paying for the fifty-year failure of atomic power, it is now the pretext for cash windfalls that would stagger even J.P. Morgan.

It has been an astonishing coup.

Or so it would seem.

Chapter Eight:
The Last Energy War

AB1890 epitomized turn-of-the-millennium corporate greed and power.

It rode the deregulatory wave that has transformed the airline, trucking and telecommunications industries. It genuflected to the Reaganesque demand that business "get government off its back" by ending bothersome regulations.

But it let those very corporations feed mightily at the public trough, twisting their bad nuclear investments into, as Nader puts it, "the biggest corporate welfare handout in U.S. history."

Except between public and private power, there's been scant competition in the electricity business since the chaotic 1880s. The fortress of regulated monopolies, in place for roughly a century, is now being transformed into a phalanx of deregulated monopolies.

For the IOUs, there remains the burden of the reactors themselves, and their wastes. The cost of managing dead nukes, and of dealing with spent fuel and other radioactive offal, is a massive question mark. No one knows how much decommissioning will cost. Nor, amidst bitter battles over the proposed national dump at Yucca Mountain, Nevada, does anyone know the price of dealing with spent fuel, or where it will go.

Or who will pay the tab. The IOUs and the public are at permanent odds over final liability for the countless billions it may take to bury the Peaceful Atom.

Amidst that unresolved argument, the utilities are unloading the reactors at what Paul Gunter of the Nuclear Information & Resource Service calls "yard sale prices." As they transform from power brokers to cash-rich global buccaneers, most electric CEOs want no part of risky reactors and their uncertain legacies.

In contrast, transmission is a virtual business with virtually no liabilities. So is buying and building gas plants with unregulated returns, rather than ones limited to dowdy old service areas with set profits and real responsibilities. Once they get their stranded cash windfalls, many utilities can't wait to dump their troublesome reactors.

But who will buy them?

With deregulation has come a whole new breed of "McNuke" fleet operators. Amergen, a blend of Philadelphia Electric and British Nuclear Fuels, pursued TMI One and Vermont Yankee. Entergy, from New Orleans, has bought Pilgrim and River Bend. Minnesota's Northern States Power and Bryson's Mission Energy have hinted at joining the fray.

Many nukes aren't worth even junk change. New Jersey's Oyster Creek, Com Ed's Zion 1 & 2, Michigan's Big Rock all shut unceremoniously. But for those increasingly dangerous plants with a few more years to be squeezed out, there may be the fleet operators.

By selling them, the IOUs escape to a legal gray zone.

Which corporate entity will actually deal with the wastes? Who will handle decommissioning? Who will go bankrupt in the inevitable next meltdown?

The sell-offs are a form of radioactive liability laundering. The final disposition of those waste and decommissioning liabilities becomes subject to decades of newly complicated legal wrangling. Bitter disputes are aflame over the hundreds of millions set aside in decommissioning funds, with the utilities demanding their usual tax subsidies. The public is being once again set up as the ultimate dupe.

But the public is not altogether buying.

In New Hampshire, after decades of bitter battle over Seabrook, the state legislature and PUC balked at paying for it. Its owner, Northeast Utilities, went to federal court.

In California, AB1890 was challenged at the polls. Against enormous odds, and at tremendous personal sacrifice, Herb Gunther of the Public Media Center, consumer advocate Harvey Rosenfield, the California and national Public Interest Research Groups and a host of other green/consumer groups gathered more than 700,000 signatures to force AB1890 onto the fall, 1998, ballot. With $28.5 billion at stake, Bryson, Cavanagh and their IOU cohorts marshaled an unprecedented war chest. "We had less than a million for our campaign," said Gunther. "They spent $40 million that we know of, but it will probably prove more like $80 million."

Enron ducked the fight. The natural gas conglomerate originally pushed deregulation. But stranded cost surcharges made it impossible for Enron to compete. So it should have jumped in with both feet to fight AB1890.

Instead, amidst the furor, Enron bought Oregon's Portland General Electric, with its dead Trojan reactor.

Suddenly Enron wanted stranded costs of its own. In a pathetic display of corporate myopia, it left Gunther and his cohorts fatally underfunded.

California's unions made a similar mistake. Organized labor has correctly recognized deregulation as a way for IOUs to de-unionize their transmission systems, production facilities and other working operations, cutting back on service and cutting off low income consumers. But California labor cut a deal with Diablo. Hoping to preserve reactor jobs, the California AFL-CIO backed AB1890's stranded cost bailout. (Massachusetts unions did much the same, only to see the new McNuke owner of the Pilgrim reactor move quickly toward de-unionization.)

To preserve their gigantic windfall, the California utilities called in all their chips with a wide range of labor, ethnic and community groups around the state. "If Proposition 9 passes," warned PG&E President Gordon Smith, "it's virtually certain that Diablo Canyon and San Onofre would be shut down." But if AB1890 escaped unscathed, added PG&E Vice President David Oatley, there was "a long future" for nuclear power in California.

To co-opt the green consumer opposition, the utilities used Cavanagh as their primary flack. In a last-minute torrent of cash, they buried repeal, 70-30.

But it may have been a pyrrhic victory, reminiscent of the 1976 defeat of six anti-nuke referenda (including one in California) after which the safe energy movement really erupted. In Washington, Wenonah Hauter, director of Nader's Critical Mass Energy Project, helped form Ratepayers for Affordable Green Energy (RAGE) a broad coalition quickly embraced by some 200 grassroots consumer and environmental groups nationwide.

In Massachusetts, a referendum like California's went down to well-funded defeat. But with their long history of town meeting democracy, Bay State consumers established "community choice" for towns and counties wanting to choose their own power provider. "It's public power without ownership," explains Paul Fenn of the American Power Project. "It introduces a very powerful form of democracy to the utility industry."

The clause seemed to pay quick dividends. In early 1999, twenty towns from Cape Cod and Martha's Vineyard aggregated their demand, and requested bids. They returned with a price well below the "standard offer," reaping the first real community benefits from deregulation.

But as the industry has fought grassroots attempts to win public power for more than a century, so it's thrown legal and political barriers against the Cape Light project, slowing down the process. "It's going to be a long, tough battle," says Fenn.

But a widespread one. A strong community aggregator clause was ripped out of the New Jersey deregulation bill at the last minute by a bought legislature. But in mid 1999 a dozen New Jersey towns re-started the fight for community control on their own. Parallel movements have risen up in California, including large-scale industrial co-generation around the city of Pittsburgh. In Ohio, a strong community choice provision in the state's deregulation law guarantees a long series of Tom Johnson-style energy wars.

Indeed, in the long run, community choice could be the ultimate fruit of unintended consequences, a backdoor route to the public-controlled power stymied by the private utility industry for 120 years. How far it goes will, as always, depend on how hard the public fights and how much of the money power we can overcome.

In Davis and Long Beach, California, public power activists are fighting to establish municipal utility districts. Elsewhere, church groups and political organizations, and towns like Santa Monica are skirting the anti-aggregation barriers and demanding green power, generated by wind and solar.

Ironically, so are some industries. "A lot of big users are aggregating around co-generation," says one CPUC staffer. "Even with all the utility subsidies, it looks like they'll be leaving the grid."

AB1890 and dereg laws in Ohio and other states technically require stranded cost payments even from those who generate all their own electricity. But will off-grid entities that get their power from on-site fuel cells, gas co-generators, efficiency and renewables meekly pay tribute to the dead nukes of obsolete utilities?

Meanwhile, "green marketers" push clean power produced by natural means. Those stranded cost surcharges and other barriers do make it slow going. And some of the claims are confusing and possibly false. But "clean, green power" is proving very popular. Its market future is unpredictable but potentially unlimited.

In Congress, Rep. Kucinich's bill embodies most of what green consumers want. No stranded costs. Community choice. A Renewable Portfolio Standard to guarantee that a growing percentage of our energy comes cleanly, from the sun. Consumer privacy. Protections for low-income working people, the elderly and the young. A blueprint for a clean, safe, equitable energy future.

As word has spread, state-by-state confrontations are increasingly fierce. In Pennsylvania, a consumer revolt took billions out of the stranded cost bill. In Texas and Ohio, bitter statewide battles erupted over stranded costs, community choice, renewables, co-generation, unionization—the whole gamut.

With a strong green-consumer movement and deep divisions between the utilities and industrials, grassroots advocates forced a Republican legislature to make Ohio the second state with strong community choice options. It failed to win a Renewable Portfolio Standard. But Ohio's green consumer movement did get guarantees for low income consumers and a range of other popular measures. In the century-long tradition of northern Ohio utility arrogance, FirstEnergy of Akron threatened to sue.

Meanwhile Florida and some twenty-five other states hang back, waiting to see how things sort out.

A wise move. Amidst the global-warmed summer of 1999 (the hottest on record) widespread breakdowns and blackouts led *The New York Times* to warn of "deep-seated problems at the nation's largest electric power companies." *The Times* reported on its front page that the nation's big utilities were grappling badly not only with deregulation, but with "aging and long-neglected equipment, new and sometimes confusing transmission networks and unprecedented demands for electricity to power the technology behind a booming economy."

In short, having devoted a century of greed to cutting corners and resisting public control, and 50 years to beating back renewables and efficiency, the IOUs have stuck the nation with a shoddily maintained, dangerously unreliable and increasingly inadequate infra-structure, poised at the brink of catastrophe.

At very least, because of cost-cutting at our remaining hundred-odd commercial reactors, deregulation increased the odds that such a catastrophe could be radioactive.

As the millennium dawns, the only firm guarantee about electric deregulation is that final resolution is uncertain—and years away. The U.S. Supreme Court will ultimately have a say. But legally and politically, as always, the business and politics of moving electrons can be counted on only to shock and transform us.

Solar and wind are still officially scorned as marginal. Fuel cells and photovoltaics are dismissed as fringe players (though far less so with each new rolling blackout). Efficiency is shunned by utility operators now back in the business of selling all the electricity they can.

But on a crowded planet, technologies operating in harmony with the natural environment must ultimately prevail. Humankind has no choice but to bring its industrial machine in sync with its natural life support systems.

In the long run, green technologies are invariably the cheapest and most creative of jobs. For a nation that still wastes half its energy, the first step—towards efficiency—should be obvious. On the supply side, true to Barry Commoner's vision, methane is already the least expensive, most versatile fuel for electricity generation. Unless it is biologically produced, natural gas does have very serious ecological impacts. But along with wind power, it could force shut every coal, oil and nuclear generator now operating. Only the political power of a technologically obsolete utility oligopoly keeps those old burners pouring out their pollutants.

But the fifty-year radioactive wrong turn away from the sun is winding down. Ultimately, electric power generation will be done by natural means, if for no other reason than our ecological survival depends on it.

Likewise the politics of deregulation.

If the inevitability of technological revolution is the first reality of a new age in energy, the power of a grassroots movement to force it ahead is the second.

The Twentieth Century has been laden with failures of the public will. The American consumer has been beaten, gouged, manipulated and poisoned by the big utilities ever since Brush and Edison threw those first switches.

But we've also won our share. For all its set-backs, the No Nukes movement helped limit Richard Nixon's nightmare of 1000 U.S. reactors by the year 2000 to just 104, and counting downward. It has conducted hundreds of electoral campaigns, referenda, rallies, demonstrations and mass arrests with only a handful of serious injuries, an astonishing record to maintain through a quarter-century of active confrontation in a society so thoroughly laden with violence and cynicism.

It helps that as the new millennium dawns, there is no mystery about what we need for a safe, sane energy future. As advanced by Sen. George Norris and President Truman's Paley Commission, by the solar blueprints of Lovins and Commoner, by the nonviolent activism of the No Nukes alliances, by the on-going campaigns of Nader and RAGE and by scores of local grassroots groups, the final formula is simple:

➤ End nuclear power.

➤ Phase-out coal and oil, with methane soon to be organically produced.

➤ Utility companies must foot the bill for their own failed investments, nuclear and otherwise;

➤ Communities must be able to choose their own power suppliers, both by price and by method of generation.

➤ Spread renewable and efficient technologies that work in harmony with nature rather than at war with it, and that are owned and operated by the people that use them, with cost accounting methods that include health, ecological and aesthetic impacts.

Given the failure of the IOUs to innovate, given the horrifying realities of Chernobyl and Three Mile Island, given the threat of global warming and a destroyed ozone layer, and given the poisoning of our air and water—we have no choice.

Future historians may note that it was the IOUs themselves that opened the Pandora's Box of their own demise. Deregulation may look good now to monopolists grabbing at those huge short-term profits and looting those decommissioning funds.

But they're also throwing some heavily charged dice.

We know that our ecological and economic survival are at stake. We know what we need, and what is technologically available.

We've experienced enough grassroots success to have a clear idea of how to get it.

Now we need to do just that. While there's still time.

Appendix

Various Comments on Stranded Costs

"The due process clause of the Fourteenth Amendment...does not insure to public utilities the right under all circumstances to have a return upon the value of the property so used. The loss of, or the failure to obtain patronage, due to competition, does not justify the imposition of charges that are exorbitant and unjust to the public. The clause of the Constitution here invoked does not protect public utilities against business hazards."
—Public Utilities Commission of Montana v. Great Northern Utilities, U.S. Supreme Court, U.S. 130, 135 (1933).

"The Fifth Amendment does not provide utility investors with a haven from the operation of market forces."—Judge Kenneth Starr, Jersey Central Power & Light v. FERC, DC Circuit (1987).

"Stranded cost is a utility term. In economics, [it's] called uneconomic assets. And in Economics 101 those sunk costs get written off. There's no rocket science involved."—Richard Abdoo, CEO of Wisconsin Electric

Power, testifying before the House Energy and Power Subcommittee, July, 1994.

"It is simply bad government policy to write multi-billion dollar checks to large corporations and then make consumers pick up the tab. In most states, policy makers are all too willing to hand inefficient utilities a big bag of cash at the starting gate of competition." —The Heritage Foundation, August 7, 1997.

"Under the California 'deregulation' scheme, billions of dollars of ratepayer money has been committed, not to a sustainable energy future but to the outright bailout of uneconomic nuclear and fossil fuel plants owned by investors, plants that ratepayers have already paid billions of dollars to maintain."—David Brower

Sources and Organizations

This book's short format precludes a full footnote section. For specific references, or to make comments, ask questions or whatever, please contact me at <nonukeshw@aol.com>, or at 1160 W. Broad, Columbus, OH 43222-1317.

Overall, some key sources for this book include:

Books

Dan Berman and John O'Connor, *Who Owns the Sun?* (White River Junction, VT: Chelsea Green, 1996).

Daniel Ford, *The Cult of the Atom* (NY: Touchstone, 1982).

Mark Hertsgaard, *Nuclear Inc.* (NY: Pantheon, 1983).

Richard Munson, *The Power Makers* (Emmaus, PA: The Rodale Press, 1985).

Peter Pringle and James Spigelman, *The Nuclear Barons* (NY: Holt, 1981).

Ray Reece, *The Sun Betrayed* (Boston: South End Press, 1979).

Richard Rudolph and Scott Ridley, *Power Struggle* (NY: Harper & Row, 1986)

Harvey Wasserman's History of the United States (NY: Four Walls, Eight Windows, 1989).

Reports

Charles Komanoff and Cora Roelofs, *Fiscal Fission: The Economic Failure of Nuclear* (DC: Greenpeace, 1992).

Safe Energy Communication Council, *The Great Ratepayer Robbery* (DC: SECC, 1998).

Articles

Savannah Blackwell, "The Private Energy Elite," *San Francisco Bay Guardian*, October 8, 1997.

James Cook, "Nuclear Follies," *Forbes Magazine*, February, 1985.

Peter Kaplan, "California 'Fiasco' Worries Regulators," *Washington Times*, August 3, 1998.

Kathryn Kranhold, "Edison's Environmentalist CEO Faces Questions from Green Critics," *Wall Street Journal*, January 12, 1999.

Brian O'Reilly, "Transforming the Power Business," *Fortune* Magazine, September 29, 1997.

Rebecca Smith, "Deregulation No Boon to the Public," *Sacramento Bee*, June 15, 1997.

Harvey Wasserman, "Inherit the Wind," *The Nation*, June 16, 1997.

ACTIVIST CONTACTS

Grassroots groups are fighting (effectively) for safe energy and public power throughout the world. Contact:

AMERICAN LOCAL POWER PROJECT
1615 Broadway, Oakland, CA.
510-451-1727
www.local.org

AMERICAN PUBLIC POWER ASSOCIATION
2301 M St. NW, Washington, DC 20037-1484
202-467-2900
www.appanet.org.

CITIZEN AWARENESS NETWORK
Box 83, Shlbourne Fall, MA 01370
CAN@shaysnet.com.

NUCLEAR INFORMATION AND RESOURCE SERVICE
1424 16th NW, Washington, DC 20036
202-328-0002
www.nirsnet.org.

RATEPAYERS FOR AFFORDABLE GREEN ENERGY (RAGE)
c/o Critical Mass Energy Project of Public Citizen
215 Pennsylvania SE, Washington, DC, 20003
202-546-4996.
www.citizen.org.

SAFE ENERGY COMMUNICATION COUNCIL
1717 Massachusetts NW, Washington, DC 20036
202-483-8491.
www.safeenergy.org.

U.S. PUBLIC INTEREST RESEARCH GROUP
218 D SE, Washington DC 20003
202-546-9707

HARVEY WASSERMAN has been called "perhaps the best-known reporter on nuclear topics" (by the *S.F. Review of Books*). *New Age Journal* says "Harvey Wasserman has staked a valid claim to the long-unfulfilled position of historian for a new, emerging generation. Author of *Harvey Wasserman's History of the United States*, four other books and innumerable articles and essays, he has been writing, speaking and organizing worldwide on energy issues since 1973. His "Sixth Column" appears bi-weekly in the Columbus (Ohio) *Alive*. He is also senior advisor to the Nuclear Information and Resource Service.

Other Books by Harvey Wasserman:

Harvey Wasserman's History of the United States (New York: Four Walls, Eight Windows, 1989).

America Born & Reborn (New York: MacMillan, 1984).

Energy War: Reports from the Front (Westport, CT.: Lawrence Hill, 1979).

Killing Our Own: The Disaster of America's Experience with Atomic Radiation (New York: Dell/Delta, 1982). With Norman Solomon, Robert Alvarez and Eleanor Walters.

Portland Community College Libraries